Woodland Sketches,
Sea Pieces, Fireside Tales
and New England Idyls

Edward MacDowell

Woodland Sketches, Sea Pieces, Fireside Tales and New England Idyls

DOVER PUBLICATIONS, INC.
Mineola, New York

Bibliographical Note

This Dover edition, first published in 2012, is a new compilation of works, originally published separately as follows: *Woodland Sketches,* Arthur P. Schmidt, Boston and New York, 1899; *Sea Pieces,* Arthur P. Schmidt, 1898; *Fireside Tales,* Arthur P. Schmidt, 1902; and *New England Idyls,* Arthur P. Schmidt, 1902.

International Standard Book Number

ISBN-13: 978-0-486-48586-7
ISBN-10: 0-486-48586-2

Manufactured in the United States by LSC Communications
48586204   2019
www.doverpublications.com

Contents

Woodland Sketches, Op. 51

I.

To a Wild Rose.

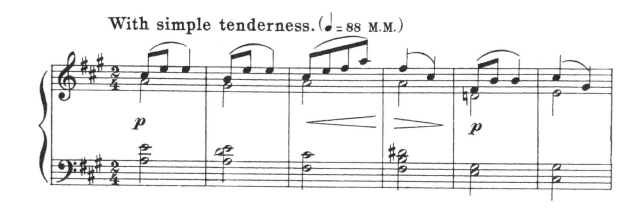

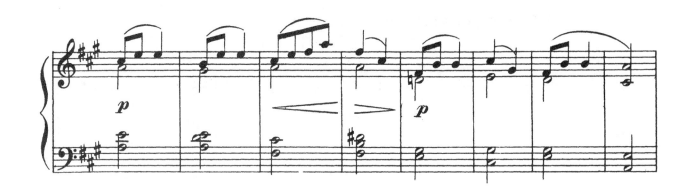

II.
Will o' the Wisp.

Swift and light; fancifully. (♩. = 116)

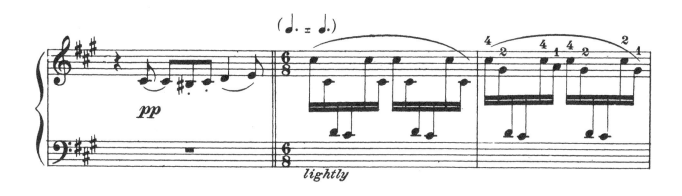

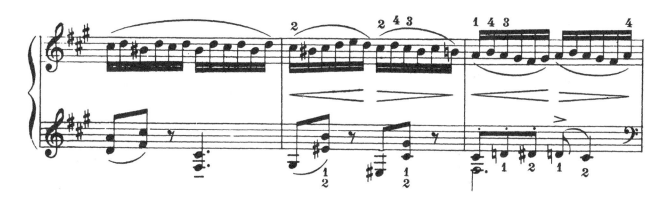

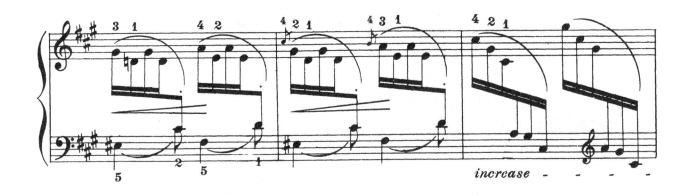

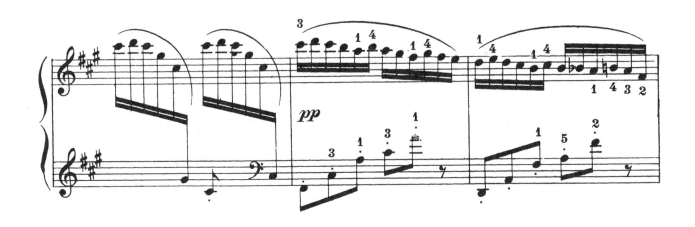

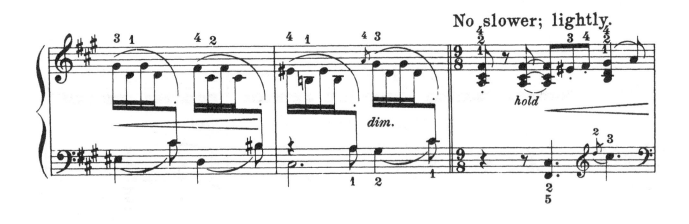

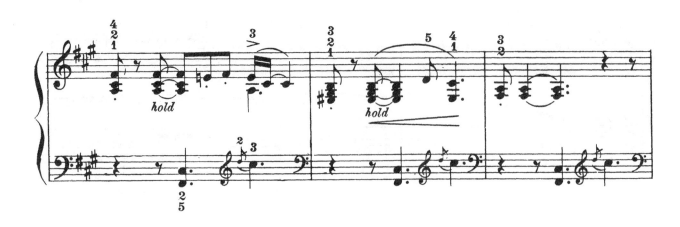

III.
At an old Trysting-place.

Somewhat quaintly; not too sentimentally. ($\bigcirc$ = 48)

IV.
In Autumn.

Buoyantly, almost exuberantly. ($\bullet$ = 132)

V.

From an Indian Lodge.

*) The low notes of the octaves carry the melody

*) The upper notes of the octaves carry the melody *p* etc.

ppp

VI.

To a Water-lily.

In dreamy, swaying rhythm. ($\textstyle\frac{}{}$ = 52)

The accompaniment very softly throughout

with pedal

Questioningly.

soft and liquid in tone

increase -

gradually increase and accelerate -

VII.

From Uncle Remus.

With much humor; joyously. ($\quad$ = 126)

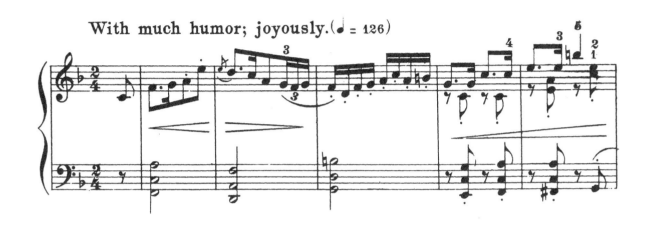

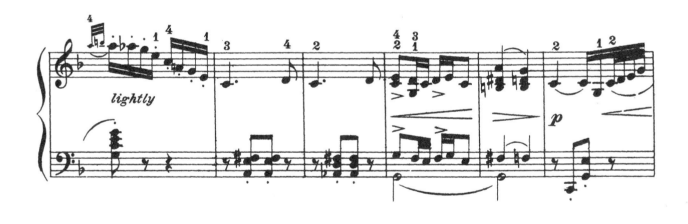

VIII.

A Deserted Farm.

IX.
By a Meadow Brook.

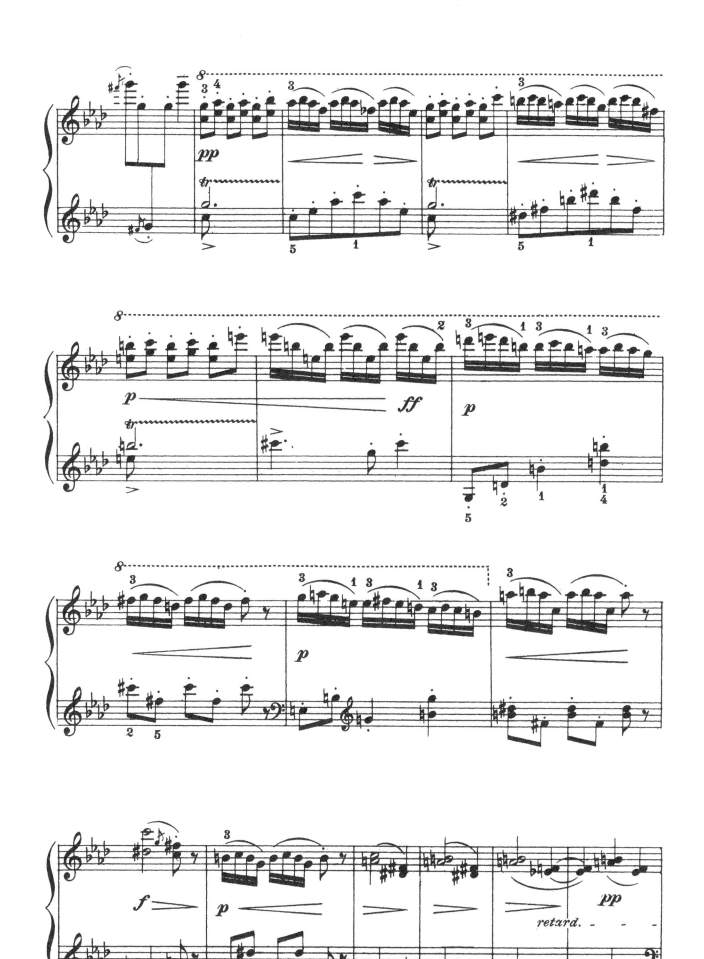

X.
Told at Sunset.

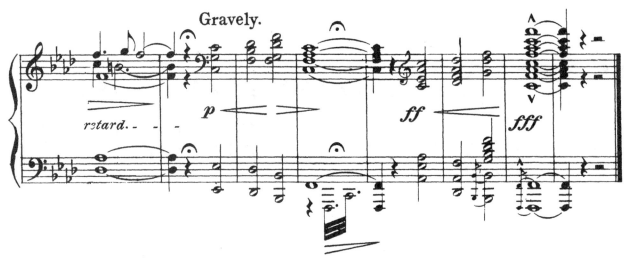

Sea Pieces, Op. 55

To the Sea.

"Ocean thou mighty monster."

With dignity and breadth. (♩ = 66.)

From a Wandering Iceberg.

An errant princess of the north,
A virgin, snowy white
Sails adown the summer seas
To realms of burning light.

A.D. MDCXX.

The yellow setting sun
Melts the lazy sea to gold
And gilds the swaying galleon
That towards a land of promise
Lunges hugely on.

In unbroken rolling rhythm. (♩. = 58.)

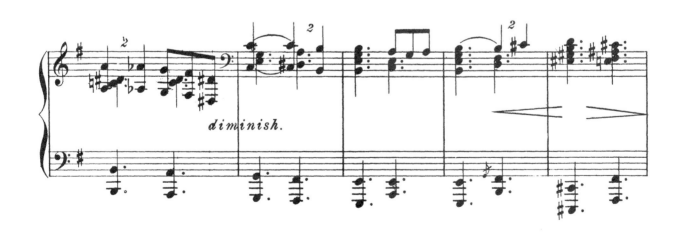

Sturdily and sternly, but without

change of rhythm.

Starlight.

The stars are but the cherubs
That sing about the throne
Of gray old Ocean's spouse,
Fair Moon's pale majesty.

★) Chords marked ⌐ are not to be rolled.

Song.

A merry song, a chorus brave,
And yet a sigh regret
*For roses sweet, in woodland lanes_*
Ah, love can ne'er forget!

In changing moods.

From the Depths.

"And who shall sound the mystery of the sea?"

In languid swaying rhythm. (♩ = 48.)

Nautilus.

"A fairy sail and a fairy boat."

In Mid-Ocean.

Inexorable!
  Thou straight line of eternal fate
That ring'st the world,
  Whil'st on thy moaning breast
We play our puny parts
  And reckon us immortal!

Fireside Tales, Op. 61

AN OLD LOVE STORY.

OF BR'ER RABBIT.

FROM A GERMAN FOREST.

With deep feeling, dreamily. (♩ = about 40.)

OF SALAMANDERS.

A HAUNTED HOUSE.

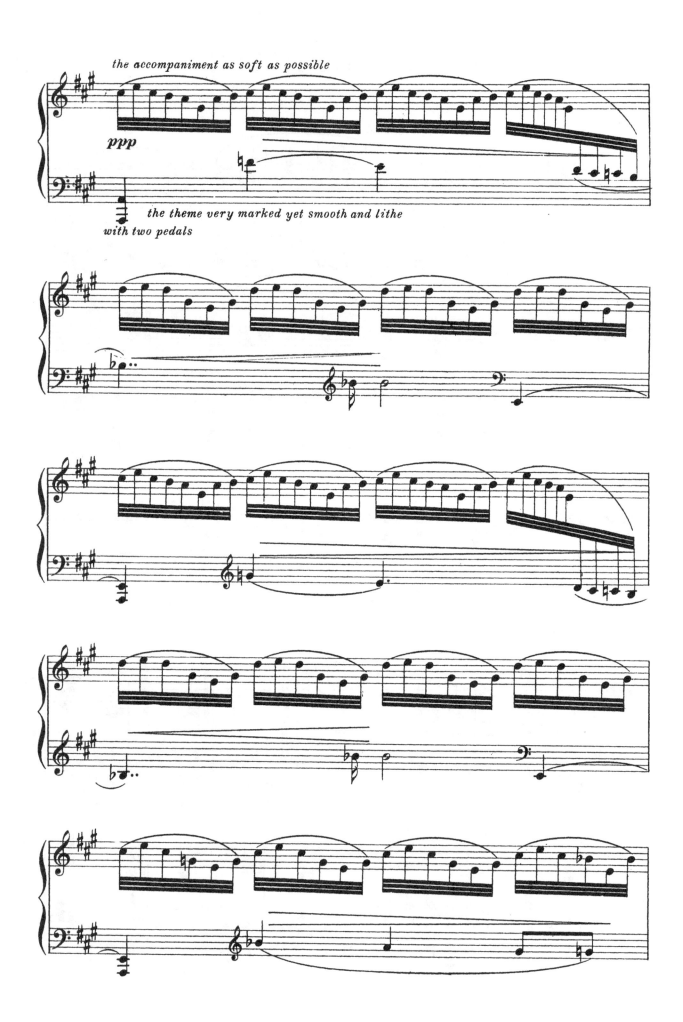

leave 2d ped.

BY SMOULDERING EMBERS.

New England Idyls, Op. 62

I.

AN OLD GARDEN.

Sweet - alyssum,
    Moss grown stair,
Rows of roses,
    Larkspur fair.

All old posies,
    Tokens rare
Of love undying
    Linger there.

Simply, tenderly. (♩ = about 80.)

With pedal.

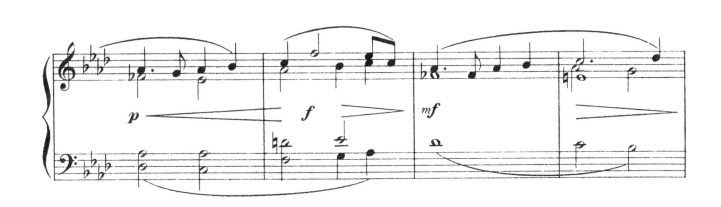

II.

MID-SUMMER.

Droning Summer slumbers on
Midst drowsy murmurs sweet.
Above, the lazy cloudlets drift,
Below, the swaying wheat.

III.

MID-WINTER.

In shrouded awe the world is wrapped,
The sullen wind doth groan,
Neath winding-sheet the earth is stone,
The wraiths of snow have flown.

And lo! a thread of fate is snapped,
A breaking heart makes moan;
A virgin cold doth rule alone
From old Mid-winter's throne.

IV.

WITH SWEET LAVENDER.

From days of yore,
Of lover's lore,
A faded bow
Of one no more.

A treasured store
Of lover's lore,
Unmeasured woe
For one, no more.

With great tenderness and delicacy. ($\quarternote$ = about 48.)

V.

IN DEEP WOODS.

Above, long slender shafts of opal flame,
Below, the dim cathedral aisles;
The silent mystery of immortal things
Broods o'er the woods at eve.

*) *Hold grace note d, with sust. pedal to the end.*

VI.

INDIAN IDYL.

Alone by the wayward flame
She weaves broad wampum skeins
While afar through the summer night
Sigh the wooing flutes' soft strains.

VII.

TO AN OLD WHITE PINE.

A giant of an ancient race
He stands, a stubborn sentinel
O'er swaying, gentle forest trees
That whisper at his feet.

Gravely, with dignity. ($\quad$ = about 84.)

VIII

FROM PURITAN DAYS.

"In Nomine Domini."

With measured emphasis. (o = about 54)

IX.

FROM A LOG CABIN.

A house of dreams untold,
It looks out over the whispering tree-tops
And faces the setting sun.

With deep feeling. (♩ = about 48.)

X.

THE JOY OF AUTUMN.

From hill-top to vale,
Through meadow and dale,
Young Autumn doth wake the world
And naught shall avail,
But our souls shall sail
With the flag of life unfurled.

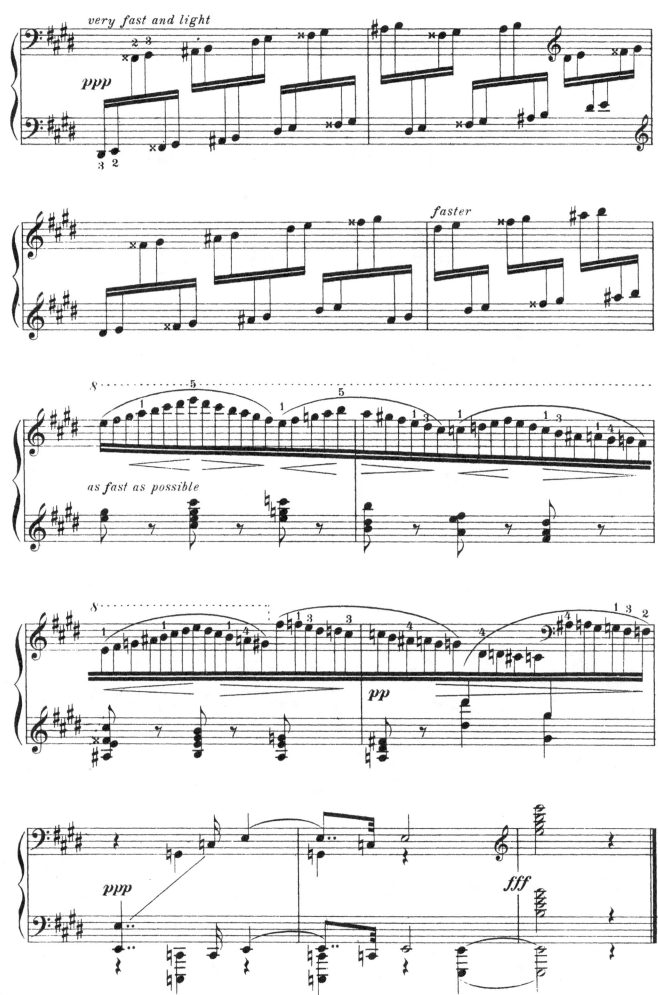